Fairy Tale Creatures

Genies

by Sophie Geister-Jones

FOCUS READERS

BEACON

www.focusreaders.com

Focus Readers is distributed by North Star Editions:
sales@northstareditions.com | 888-417-0195

Produced for Focus Readers by Red Line Editorial.

Photographs ©: Shutterstock Images, cover, 1, 4, 6, 8, 12, 14, 17, 19, 20–21, 22, 26, 29; iStockphoto, 11, 25

Library of Congress Cataloging-in-Publication Data
Names: Geister-Jones, Sophie, author.
Title: Genies : fairy tale creatures / Sophie Geister-Jones.
Description: Lake Elmo, MN : Focus Readers, [2022] | Series: Fairy tale creatures | Includes index. | Audience: Grades 2-3
Identifiers: LCCN 2021006317 (print) | LCCN 2021006318 (ebook) | ISBN 9781637390023 (hardcover) | ISBN 9781637390092 (paperback) | ISBN 9781637390160 (ebook) | ISBN 9781637390221 (pdf)
Subjects: LCSH: Jinn--Juvenile literature.
Classification: LCC GR549 .G45 2022 (print) | LCC GR549 (ebook) | DDC 297.2/17--dc23
LC record available at https://lccn.loc.gov/2021006317
LC ebook record available at https://lccn.loc.gov/2021006318

Printed in the United States of America
Mankato, MN
082021

About the Author

Sophie Geister-Jones lives in Saint Paul, Minnesota. She enjoys reading and watching her friends do puzzles while she eats food.

Table of Contents

Chapter 1

A Magic Lamp

A young boy stumbled across the desert. A strong wind whipped up clouds of sand. Squinting his eyes, the boy spotted a cave. He ran inside to escape the storm.

Caves can provide people shelter from sandstorms.

In some stories, genies appear when people rub the sides of lamps.

The boy walked through a narrow tunnel. Suddenly, the tunnel widened. A large room lay up ahead. Treasure covered its floor.

The boy took a step toward the treasure. But he tripped over a lamp on the ground.

The boy picked up the lamp. He wiped its side with his sleeve. Smoke poured from the lamp, and a huge genie appeared. The genie thanked the boy for freeing him. He gave the boy a wish as a reward.

Fun Fact

In addition to lamps, genies can be trapped in jewelry, pots, or jars.

Chapter 2

Varied Versions

Genies are based on tales of creatures called jinn. Jinn come from Arab **mythology**. They are **invisible**. And they can do magic. Stories of jinn are very old. People told them out loud for many years.

Stories of jinn date back to at least 2400 BCE.

The stories changed and spread over time. Later, some of them were written down.

Many books tell stories of jinn. *One Thousand and One Nights* is a famous example. This book is a collection of stories. The stories came from Asia, North Africa, and the Middle East. People gathered

Fun Fact

Jinn are mentioned in the Quran. This is the holy book of Islam.

One main story links all the tales in *One Thousand and One Nights*. A woman tells the tales to a king.

the stories together. They also made new versions.

In the 1700s, Antoine Galland **translated** the stories into French. He used the word *génie* to refer to jinn. He also added some stories.

People changed stories about genies to reflect their own cultures and ideas.

One was "Aladdin and the Magic Lamp." In this story, a boy finds a lamp. A genie is inside. The genie helps Aladdin. He grants wishes for the boy.

Many people read Galland's book. It shaped how the stories spread.

In the original stories, most jinn were free and powerful. But stories in Europe began to change. They were more like Galland's stories. For example, they used the word *genie*. And they had genies serve people and grant wishes. However, the genies could still be tricky.

Fun Fact

In early versions, the story of Aladdin took place in China. Later versions changed the setting.

Chapter 3

Changing Shape

Both jinn and genies are invisible most of the time. But people do sometimes see them. Jinn often show up to trick people. They have the power to shape-shift. They can take the form of many animals.

Genies and jinn can take many different forms.

Snakes are common choices. So are lions and wolves. Jinn can also choose to look like humans.

Most genies appear when people find or call them. Many genies are trapped in objects, such as lamps or bottles. The object's owner controls the genie.

An owner can make the genie do magic. But the owner must guard the object carefully. If someone else takes it, the genie will belong to that person instead.

Rings can give people the power to control genies.

In contrast, jinn are usually wild and free. Some stay away from people. They live in lonely places, such as deserts or **ruins**. Others live in or near people's homes. In some cases, jinn get trapped in objects.

These jinn can sometimes be controlled by humans.

One story tells of a king who captured many jinn. He kept them in jars. He made them build and fight for him. He became rich and powerful.

Many years later, a man was fishing. He found one of the jars. He

Fun Fact

In some stories, people cast spells to control jinn.

Some legends say jinn live in caves in the desert.

opened it. One of the jinn appeared. He tried to kill the man. But the man tricked him. The man got him to go back into the jar.

STORY SPOTLIGHT

Why So Blue?

Today, images of genies show them with blue skin. But that wasn't always the case. The movie *Aladdin* helped make this coloring popular. Disney made *Aladdin* in the 1990s. The movie used colors as **symbols**. Reds and oranges meant bad. Blues and greens meant good.

The genie helped Aladdin. So, artists made him blue. This color told viewers he was a good character. Later in the movie, a bad character turns into a genie. That genie is red. The colors made it easy for viewers to tell who was good and who was bad.

A man dresses up as a genie coming from a lamp.

RHOL
Moser

Chapter 4

Magical Powers

In early stories, jinn have great power. They can do magic. Stories also say they can fly or time travel. In some ways, jinn are like ghosts. They can haunt places. And they can **possess** people.

A valley in Saudi Arabia is said to be haunted by jinn.

Sometimes they even appear in people's dreams.

Jinn can use their powers for good or evil. Bad jinn can make people sick. Other jinn heal people.

Some jinn guard treasure. They may hurt people who try to take it. Or they can give it away. But first, they often make people pass a test.

Fun Fact

Legends say jinn are most active at dusk.

Jinn may guard treasure that is hidden in caves or buried underground.

People can ask jinn for luck or help. But they must be careful. In many stories, jinn are dangerous.

In Western stories, genies are often friendly and helpful.

They like causing trouble. They hurt or trick people. As a result, stories about them tend to be scary.

Most genies in **Western** stories have less power. Many genies must serve humans. Some can grant only three wishes. Problems can still come up. Wishes can have **consequences** people didn't plan on. Or genies can make mistakes. Even so, the stories tend to be less scary. They can even be funny.

Legends of genies continue to change. Sometimes legends blend together. Western ideas about genies shape movies around the world. And scary jinn appear in a few Western movies and games.

FOCUS ON

Genies

Write your answers on a separate piece of paper.

1. Write a paragraph explaining the main ideas of Chapter 2.
2. Would you rather read funny stories about genies or scary stories about jinn? Why?
3. What can jinn do that genies cannot do?
   - **A.** They can do magic.
   - **B.** They can be trapped in jars.
   - **C.** They can appear to people in dreams.
4. Why might stories change as they spread to new areas?
   - **A.** People in the new areas might use the same words.
   - **B.** People in the new areas might add their own interests and ideas.
   - **C.** All people have the same interests and ideas.

5. What does **reward** mean in this book?

*The genie thanked the boy for freeing him. He gave the boy a wish as a **reward**.*

- **A.** a plan to get back at someone
- **B.** a gift thanking someone for doing good
- **C.** a trick to make someone mad

6. What does **captured** mean in this book?

*One story tells of a king who **captured** many jinn. He kept them in jars.*

- **A.** took a picture of something
- **B.** trapped something
- **C.** let something go free

Answer key on page 32.

Glossary

consequences
The results of a choice or action.

invisible
Not able to be seen.

mythology
A culture's traditional stories that explain the world in some way.

possess
To take control of someone's body, often making the body do or say things.

ruins
Broken pieces of buildings, especially ones from very long ago.

setting
The location where a story takes place.

symbols
Things that stand for and remind people of other things or ideas.

translated
Changed from one language to another.

Western
Coming from or shaped by the people and ideas of Europe and North America.

To Learn More

BOOKS

Loh-Hagan, Virginia. *Genies*. Ann Arbor, MI: Cherry Lake Publishing, 2018.

London, Martha. *Genies*. Minneapolis: Abdo Publishing, 2020.

Sautter, A. J. *Discover Gnomes, Halflings, and Other Wondrous Fantasy Beings*. Mankato, MN: Capstone Press, 2018.

NOTE TO EDUCATORS

Visit **www.focusreaders.com** to find lesson plans, activities, links, and other resources related to this title.

Index

Answer Key: 1. Answers will vary; **2.** Answers will vary; **3.** C; **4.** B; **5.** B; **6.** B